Water Running Downhill

Rose Edition

Copyright 2015, by Joan Ellen Gage,
all rights reserved. No part of this book may be
used or reproduced by any means, graphic,
electronic, or mechanical, including photocopying,
recording, taping, or by any information storage
retrieval system without the written permission of
the publisher except in the case of brief quotations
embodied in critical articles and reviews.

The views expressed in this work are solely those
of the author and do not necessarily reflect the
views of the publisher, and the publisher hereby
disclaims any responsibility for them.

All poems and photos in this book were created by
Joan Ellen Gage and are her sole property.

Rose Macedo Kull, 11/4/1953 to 7/8/2015

Dedication

This edition of *Water Running Downhill!* is dedicated to my friend Rose. I had wanted to feature her as one of my photo creations, but, I never got to do that. So, the next best thing was to honor Rose in this book.

Rose was diagnosed with pancreatic cancer on her 60th birthday. She was a fighter, and eventually was on a monthly chemo regimen. Rose was determined to be there for her family. They lost her much too early.

So, here's to Rose, one of my heroes! I send blessings to her family, and peace to our Rose.

Acknowledgements

Thank you, my friends for being a sounding board for this book. You gave me unconditional support and helped push me out of my nest. Thanks for believing in me!

I want to thank my husband, Rob, for his patience, and for being there for me. I thank him for listening, even though he did not understand my ramblings much of the time!

And a special thank you to my Mom and Dad for your faith in me!

Table of Contents

YOUR MID-LIFE CHEERLEADER:	10
'SIS' BOOM BAH!:	11
USED GOODS:	12
WOMEN:	13
HOURGLASS BLEND:	14
MIDLIFE CLOCK:	15
IF TRUTH BE BOLD:	17
MENSES SCHMENSES:	19
BRIDE AND DOOM:	20
GREAT EXPECTATIONS:	21
WOOMAN:	22
FOOTFALLS:	24
MAGGIE & ME:	26
EIGHT IN DOG YEARS:	27

HONEY DO LIST:	29
KAREN IN THE LOOKING GLASS:	30
MIDLIFE THROUGH THE LOOKING GLASS:	31
QUARTERLY REPORT:	32
DIRECTORY ASSISTANCE:	34
NEW YEAR'S RESOLUTIONS:	35
KEEP OUT!:	36
E-MAN-CIPATION:	37
EXERCISE IN MORPHOLOGY:	38
REAL ESTATE:	39
ELISA OZLAND:	40
EXIST-STANCE:	41
ABBI-NORMAL:	42
SILVER SPURS:	44
NEW FRONTIERS:	45

COCOON:	47
CATCH 22:	49
BUDDHA ZONE:	50
THE ZONE:	51
OVERDRIVE:	52
START-LET:	54
SKIN DEEP:	55
JULIE GROWTH:	56
MEA CULPA:	57
CHANGLING:	58
BY DESIGN:	60
MY TRIBE:	62
ONE TRIBE:	63
STATE OF GRACE:	64
GIRLFRIEND:	65

FOR MERITORIOUS SERVICE:	66
WOMEN WHO SERVE:	67
WATER RUNNING DOWNHILL:	69
DENIAL:	71
MARY EMBRACING THE FIERCE:	72
FIERCE:	73
ME AND ROSE AND THE DASHBOARD JESUS:	74
ABOUT THE AUTHOR:	76

"SIS" BOOM BAH

I am your midlife cheerleader
so, chant this cheer out loud,
and sing it out with feeling
to make your sisters proud!

Be good to yourselves
cause no one else will.
Take time to nurture,
you're not over the hill!

Become the balance
quit the balancing act,
life's passing you by
and that's a fact!

Leave office work at work,
remember you exist.
You can't have too much fun,
so, put it on your list!

USED GOODS

There are no
guarantees or
refunds and
no exchanges, you
have to take it as
it is.

A slight modification
may be possible, but
beyond that, what
you see is what
you get.

There may be surface
imperfections due
to materials used, and
the contents may
have settled
during handling.

But each piece is an
individually crafted, unique
work of art, a
truly one of a kind
human being.

WOMEN

Sisters
Singers of
Sad songs
Seductresses
Strong
Saintly
Soaring
Sage
Sphinxes

Women

MIDLIFE CLOCK

Time,
too much, not enough, too
slow, too fast, forever
tick, tick, ticking
away . . .

Time,
we wish it
here, we
wish it
gone . . .

Time,
feel it trickling,
teasing through
your fingers, sifting
between
your toes . . .

You
are the hourglass, your
time is running
out, tick . . . tock . . .
Half of the sand of
your being
has dwindled away. . .

Your
vital force
diminishes as
grain by
tiny grain
your essence
erodes . . .

Wake up,
it's half-past
your life!

I F TRUTH BE BOLD

After reaching this
banner year of years, with
much preparation and
soul searching, what
have I learned?

That the experience of
living continues on. Nothing
ends that does
not set something else
into motion.

That knowledge seeking is
an on-going and
ever-changing dynamic where
one must be
consciously open-minded.

That the universe's mysteries and
her divine secrets may
remain inscrutable while they
are subject to
individual interpretation.

That each one makes
their own happiness, and
life's aging shadow is

ever lengthening.

That one must
love.

MENSES SCHMENSES

Mad
Madding
Madness
Mid
Middle
Middling
Moody
Moods

GREAT EXPECTATIONS

We all grew up with the Great American Dream,
expecting to be beautiful and rich,
expecting to marry Prince Charming,
having been breast-fed on fairy tales, and
brainwashed by happy endings.

But, many of us have been disillusioned,
perhaps having gotten pretty (or passable),
and middle classed instead,
(if you were lucky).

Prince Charming turned into
your classic balding
couch potato, sports-nut
(if you were lucky)?

Possibly, you lost out on the whole
enchilada, marriage,
house in the suburbs, 1.5 children.
Maybe you're still looking for that perfect love,
(looking to get lucky).

With the worst scenario, you
got the Great American Nightmare
instead,
(whoops, out of luck)!

WOOMAN

Women carry a heavy
burden, many of
us balance outside
employment plus the
home (more work)!
Maybe child rearing completes the
load, all at the expense of
self.

We juggle our universe while
multi-tasking, cooking,
car-pooling, shopping,
laundering, errand running,
homework instructing,
house cleaning, gardening,
etcetera, etcetera.

And get this:
society dictates that
we maintain our savvy, and our good looks
during these amazing feats.
(We usually pull this off)!
And, amazingly enough, we
are still expected to have
sex, be sexy, and stay awake.

Ironically, even though

we function, on a daily basis,
as CEO's and their staff, we
still haven't had
a woman President yet,
go figure?

FOOTFALLS

Women must walk
a different path
than men.
We must walk it
carefully and
cautiously,
for fear of
discovery and/or
criticism.

Our paths
take us to
alternative planes of
consciousness. They
lead us to the
oft unexplored territory
of our mind's eye.
They bring us to truth
and to sagacity.

Choose
and make
the journey unto
your soul's threshold.
Dare
to cross over
to the land of imagination and

your heart of
creativity.

Live,
love life,
morph
into enlightenment.

EIGHT IN DOG YEARS
MAGGIE & ME

EIGHT IN DOG YEARS--(AKA FIFTY)!

Here I am
stuck
in the middle
of me.

Trying to redefine
my identity at
the precipice of
midlife, i.e.,
menopause.

There
I've said it,
the "M" word,
(sounding the death knell
of youthfulness, as we know it)!

Enter the curse of middle age,
see . . .
skin sag, lines deepen
into the antithesis
of perky.

Zombies, recite the litany:
"I'm not getting older
I'm getting better,"

the Golden Years,
(such rubbish)!

Forget that tired rhetoric.
News flash, we are supposed to age,
we are not Barbie dolls,
we are people!

Let's not fear our natural metamorphosis,
may we embrace who we are, and
who we are becoming, with fortitude.
We are powerful.
We are WOMEN!

HONEY DO LIST

In menopause, will we:
ignore laws,
break jaws,
call our Maws,
pursue a lost cause,
draw straws,
grow moss,
buy gewgaws,
reflect and pause,
make crow caws,
drink hot sauce,
master DOS,
ride a hoss,
paint our paws,
build with saws,
dress in gauze,
make oohs and aahs,
experiment with faux,
or journey to Oz,
in menopause?

MIDLIFE THROUGH THE LOOKING GLASS

Check out your reflection,
the 40 (50) something body,
hold in your gut,
stand up straight,
tighten those gluts,
add the push-up bra.
Not bad, you think,
if only I could hold my breath
forever . . .

The mirror "you" would appear
perfect, (well, it would be close),
but, don't put on those glasses,
oh no!

QUARTERLY REPORT

I have a friend who tells me
that turning fifty is
like entering into the
third quarter of
your existence.

I prefer to think of it
as my autumn, which
evokes emotions attuned more
to a surrealist watercolor,
than a bright acrylic canvas.

Using either interpretation, find
that it is time to take notice,
and make time to enjoy
this mortal realm,
while you have vitality.

I refuse to take
a negative stance
on this aging thing.
We may not be able to beat it
but we can't just submit.

We've got to harness the
power of our minds,

keep our bodies fit and lean,
feed our heads,
and keep moving forward.

There will be plenty of time
for bingo and mahjong,
if that is what you choose.
Let's try to stall the inevitable,
what have you got to lose?

DIRECTORY ASSISTANCE

Sisters, I write to you today,
my words formed from
the clarity
I now find within me.

You can label these words
bad poetry if you want,
at least I have the
guts to reach out to you!

I enlist your services in
helping you to find you, to
tap into the inner self, and
find your true heart.

Perhaps you won't receive
this wake-up call yet,
could it be your number is unlisted? Or
is your voice mail full, again?

NEW YEAR'S RESOLUTIONS

We have a new year,
they seem to be arriving at
lightning speed in
this new decade.

Think of this year as
an opportunity to
grow and celebrate, to
toast the women you have become.

Forget the past mistakes, and
focus on what makes you
content and joyous,
be your own best friend.

Live life now, not later,
for later may not
be here for you.

E-MANCIPATION

Is <u>men</u>opause
a pause from men,
or time for a woman
to stop and breathe in,
by taking <u>men</u>tal routes
for themselves
where men must keep out?

In man-less awareness
may a woman look within,
be introspective and assess. She
must take inventory
of her life and soul,
envision the future,
reach out for new goals.

Until we ponder our fate, and
unleash our lives,
our growth will stagnate, and
never embrace alive.

Though the wonder that we seek
and we very rarely find,
is hidden within the confines
of our convoluted minds.

EXERCISE IN MORPHOLOGY

Hush.
be very still,
with eyes closed,
and imagine you are
as a blank, white canvas,
a page not yet written upon.

Concentrate
on this image
within your mind,
then use this background
to paint who you truly are,
using previous life as a guideline.

Envision
the beautiful being
that you have within you,
sculpt and recreate yourself,
with your dreams as the bones,
then flesh out the rest by sheer will.

Live who you want to be!

REAL ESTATE

We are the architects of our lives,
every decision determines
the structure and shape
of our fortresses.

Sound thinking
is the mortar and brick;
sense and sensibility,
are the cornerstones.

Music, art, and creativity
provide color and texture,
while joy and happiness
bring us comfort.

Families and friends
are our treasures, and
love is the warm fire
in our heart's home.

EXIST-STANCE

Meditate on this
if you do not make an effort
to live in the moment
you will not truly
live

To always plan
for tomorrow land
ignoring the boring minutia
you will never exist
in today

To chase after
what may be
one loses
the ability
to be

ABBI-NORMAL

How did I get to be normal?
I spent my life being a square peg,
shy, funny, a brave coward.

I never wanted to go along for the ride,
always the individual, the
rebel, resisting the status quo.

I was a little late for Vietnam, or I
told myself, I would have protested,
I was the flower child, moccasins and all.

The 9 to 5 grind, and the pressures of
the working world have molded me,
rounding my prickly edges, somewhat.

I have sensible clothes, tailored and proper,
for work and the occasional event.
Mainly, I have sturdy jeans and tees.

I'm starting a renaissance of myself,
beginning with my closet.
I am exorcising dull and boring,
(goodbye brown, hello purple)!

I've got my 'cool' back,

it was just misplaced,
not forgotten.

I may be a funky, aging hippie, but
I have style! I love
being this quietly outrageous person.
One must be true to one's own self,
this I accept, and applaud, loudly.

Don't be a cookie cutter image of anyone,
find your true colors, then
step into the unique garment of yourself!

NEW FRONTIERS

I have to say that
the women I meet these days, as
peers and otherwise,
are smart and savvy.
They are really out there
breaking up the male empire
and enjoying it.

This sisterhood of women
is such a positive force, and
whether we realize it, or
not, the truth is,
women are changing
their worlds, and
it is apparent to them.

Even if the rest of the planet cannot
see this alteration,
it does not matter. It is
our own perception that does.
Women have visualized
a new reality, and made it theirs,
they now operate within this new order.

We are cowgirls of
the new frontier,
making and breaking up rules,

we ride bareback into
dangerous deserts, canyons,
and boardrooms,
while twirling our iPhones.

And, when we wear our silver spurs,
they haven't got
a chance!

COCOON

Creating calm
in your life
is as essential
to your existence
as oxygen

We have become
hurried harried
hustling husks
we have forgotten
to breathe

Nullify the noise of
modern life
shipwreck yourself
on your island aerie
nurture your native side

Unplug the phone
cut off your cell
become incommunicado
turn off the tube
acquiesce to quiet

Bask as bird song
blends with the
beating of your heart

knowingly choose to be
a universe of one

Then
gratified and grounded
will your authentic
sated-self slip
into your cocoon
of silence

CATCH-22

When are you
going to stop being
the victim?

It's not just your lot in
life, you know,
it is a cognizant choice.

You choose to believe
that you are inferior,
you don't know your worth.

If you could see the
beautiful person that I see,
you would fall in love with you.

THE ZONE

While sequestered as a willing tenant in
your self-made prison of busyness
dream of ways
you can be free

To give yourself the gift of
a precious few moments
no distractions
lock out your outer life and meditate

Find that it is almost a new experience
as you may have forgotten the sensation
of pure awareness
and nothing else

So used to being the amazing balancing act
you've found it hard to stop doing and planning
and just become still

Discover that one can see so much clearer
when traveling at
the speed of now

OVERDRIVE

I cannot ignore
the erratic beating
of my heart
or the anxiety
the tightness
surrounding my chest

Hormones abound
the pressure in my skull
accelerates the estrogen vice
winding tighter still

Testosterone easily
inflames my temper
my patience level
is at low tide

I awake in the middle
of the night with my steaming
teakettle-head boiling
ready to whistle

My body battles me to
size up and up
I fight the fight daily
or I will lose it

Calm and quiet beckon
like a siren's song
I crave down time
like an addict craves
their addiction

START-LET

Tell me, did you get to be
what you wanted to be
when you grew up?

Did you get that dream job,
were you discovered like the
gossip-rags claimed you'd be?

Are you still that plain Jane
working at the same old job
you told yourself was only temporary?

Things may not have moved on for you,
your life may be like stagnant water
with no flow, no progress, no future.

You could convince yourself
that it's not too late, and
free yourself from your drab subsistence.

You might ask yourself, again,
"what do I want to be, when I grow up?"
There is still time to find your purpose.

There is still time to find you.

SKIN DEEP

Worked into a frenzied froth of
slick soap bubbles,
water beads up on
new, born-again
baptized skin.

Late afternoon light refracts
through liquid droplets, as
water flows across my chest, and
dives downward, arcing
into my belly-button, creating
a myriad of prismatic effects.

As layers of soapy pollutants, from
daily stress, anger, and rudeness,
(man's inhumanity to woman),
are scrubbed away; whirling
and spinning, exfoliated cells careen
down the drain.

I shed my workweek
false skin; my
psyche feels resuscitated as
I evolve,
once more becoming
human, for the weekend.

GROWTH

JULIE, MEASURING UP!

MEA CULPA

I have not come this far
in my life
without making some mistakes
they are too numerous to list

If I were in a ten-step program
I would have to write letters
apologizing for the harm
that I had caused others

We must accept the blame
for our own actions
everything negative that happens to us
is <u>not</u> our parents' fault

Facing up to life's consequences
is a step on the road
to your self-recovery
don't linger in failure
move forward

CHANGLING

If you could be anywhere else
traveling for parts unknown, or known,
where would you go?
Would you inform the authorities,
or just simply disappear,
remaining a mystery to those left behind?
Such a romantic notion.

Think about it,
you could live in a jungle,
you Tarzana, (or Jane),
or become a cowgirl
riding and roping, sleeping under the stars.
How about becoming a film star
like in Hollywood's heyday?

Don't forget your old friend fantasy,
it can take you away,
and help you plan your escape.
If you imagine and envision it,
your dream may be realized, as
in your mind's eye,
it is conceived and delivered,
with you as your own midwife.

Nothing happens in this world

without your own support.
Either consciously or unconsciously,
you let the stream of life pass by,
or dive in as a willing participant.

Choose to struggle and rebuild,
or accept defeat, as the living dead.
Do not lie down quietly; resurrect yourself!

BY DESIGN

What is a breast?
It is, by design, in its simplest form,
a source of nourishment,
a literal fountain of youth.

A breast is an ornament
of the flesh, ascetically varied,
rounded, pillowed, or arched,
an achingly beautiful sculpture of nature.

A breast is a haven
for comforting small humans
or sheltering family and friends,
with arms and bodies enfolded tightly, as in prayer.

A breast can also give or receive
pleasure, with our partners,
as active participants
in the mating dance of life.

A breast is the epitome of the heart
of womankind, as with our breasts,
we nurture, comfort, and love.
That is why we hold them so dear.

Through breast cancer, women may

lose these deeply personal pieces
of their flesh, that share so much,
and give succor to life.

But, we must remember that
women are the origin of strength
in this world, and with or
without breasts, we are the same!

We will still nurture,
we will still comfort,
and we will still love.
We will do this, by design.

For Tina and all of her sisters

ONE TRIBE

Have you felt
with passing years
a more pressing
need to connect
with other women,
to share observations
and laughter,
to offer advice
or garner wisdom?
Do you feel drawn
as if by a magnetic force
to be with your own kind?

For these women
are a tribe, your tribe.
No one else will ever
understand your struggle
as they will.
Women are our people,
when we come together
we feel a oneness,
a sisterhood united.

When we come together,
we are at home.

STATE OF GRACE

I send this message
out to you
grasp it
let it define you
live it
take it to heart

The revelation is that
this is the moment
the present, and
nothing else exists

Be here
seize the now

Be your bliss
and therefore
you shall be
blessed

GIRLFRIEND

Friend of mine
there is purpose
in your sadness
you will find strength
in your struggle

There is no growth
without discomfort
we do not learn
without some pain
you will gain power
from this experience

Persevere and pursue
your karma

Your fate
is within
your own heart

WOMEN WHO SERVE

Daily, they bring me stories
of their lives and loves, their joys,
and their tragedies.
These tales speak to me
on a very personal
level, as their stories
may evolve to include mine.

These women tell me
of lives spent caring
for everyone, beginning
with raising children, encompassing
perhaps twenty years, and of being
a helpmate to their spouses,
often working elsewhere, while doing
the never-ending household chores.

But, these years of childrearing
were many times followed with
the care-taking of these women's
failing parents, a role reversal where
the parents seemed to become
the children. This was
a difficult duty, but it was a duty
done out of love.

Lastly, the women spoke of

the deterioration of their spouses.
Many of these women had no funds for outside
help, and were often frail themselves.
But they bravely served
at their spouses' sides
and offered up their
often-thankless support,
waging a war until the end.

There are no purple hearts
for care-giving, and no memorials.
This is the reality of women's lives,
this may become your existence
and mine.
Please, learn by this lesson,
this is our time,
fly and be free!

WATER RUNNING DOWNHILL!

I see my life
like water running
downhill, believing
each precious droplet
is a moment lost to me.

For a time
my essence flowed
calmly, evenly
in gentle
creeks and rivulets.

Then tiny streams
became ever-widening rivers,
time cascaded, spiraled
into whitewater rapids,
downward, rushing downward,
Niagara Falls!

After the thundering crescendo, and
as the course of my being
tapers, eventually becoming
an evaporating trickle,
I will remember the deluge fondly,
while coming to terms with
the imprint of my past life, knowing,
my destiny awaits me like the river bed

awaits the raging river.

I see my life
like water running downhill.
I see my life.

DENIAL

Is not a river in Egypt
or so I am told.

So, get out and dance
to your music.
Do it before you're too old!

MARY EMBRACING THE 'FIERCE'

Fierce

Can you do it?
Can you embrace the fierce,
bring it to the surface
of your being?

Your wounded warrior heart
beats, it has survived
in spite of you.

It is time to claim
this aspect of yourself,
to integrate it into your existence.

We are all Viking daughters,
armed, ready to do battle,
surrendering to no one,
not even ourselves.

The ancient one lies within.
Awaken her.
Awaken the power
Of your fierce warrior self.

ME AND ROSE AND THE DASHBOARD JESUS

It is 1971, Rose and I are riding in Dad's
old blue Galaxy 500, with buckle seatbelts,
windows open, no a/c, Florida
heat pours in. We don't care, we are
singing at the top of our lungs,
Neil Diamond's *Cracklin' Rosie*, Rose's song.

Rose was a timid Catholic girl with a
Long 'Giland' accent; she was shyer than me.
We borrowed each other's clothes to
widen our wardrobes.
I was taller, Rose curvier, but
we wore the same size.

We would take her dad's car, and drive
to Fort Lauderdale Beach. Rose had
a real tan; mine was mostly QT.
I could never resist turning the dashboard Jesus
around, Rose would roll her eyes,
"he wants to see where he's going," I insisted!

We were seniors, then.
We wore matching prom dresses of different hues;
mine was white, Rose's blue.
I dug out those photos last week,
after I heard the news.

There we were, captured on Kodak, frozen in time,
Cracklin' Rosie and me.

ABOUT THE AUTHOR

Joan Ellen Gage lives with her husband and their Belgian Tervuren dog, Magnolia, on their retreat in Western North Carolina. Joan had motivated and inspired dental hygiene patients for
Years while listening to their stories. This spawned
Water Running Downhill!,
Joan's first publication.

www.ingramcontent.com/pod-product-compliance
Lightning Source LLC
LaVergne TN
LVHW051511070426
835507LV00022B/3051